# Journey Back
# to the Sea

Marilyn Brookhart, LCSW

# DEDICATION

This book is dedicated to my sister, Margaret, who influenced me with metaphysical and spiritual literature as far back as Seth and Edgar Casey. Thank you, Marg, for contributing immensely to my home-grown education.

Deborah,
May you enjoy
the journey.
Peace, Love + Light
Marilyn

# Table of Contents

MARILYN BROOKHART

# *ACKNOWLEDGEMENTS*

*So many thanks to my husband and family for their tireless assistance in editing and offering their technological expertise in supporting my endeavor. I would not have been able to accomplish this without their assistance.*

MARILYN BROOKHART

## Preface-

In understanding the human journey, its purpose, its issues, its difficulties, its foibles, as well as its joys, happiness and elations, it is meaningful to look at the big picture and understand our lessons in life. Life on earth is not random, but has a grand purpose of learning and growing to our higher level of evolution. Unfortunately, if people spend more of their time and energy, fearing and deflecting and using ego defenses, such as denial, projecting, blaming and rationalizing, there is little energy or desire to create productive living and building satisfying relationships. This **self-help handbook** is designed to motivate a clearer understanding of the feared obstacles and move into a freer and less encumbered flow of life's energy.

Wisdom literature provides us with many means of accomplishing a free and easier journey to reach a good sense of inner and outer harmony. It is intended to assist those looking to diminish the struggle in life and find a more harmonious pathway to peace.

This references much of the old and new literature that offers us different modes of reaching higher enlightenment. In availing oneself of many different sources, we enable ourselves to compare and contrast and have a broader scope of understanding the journey.

Winter

## Chapter 1- The Journey Begins

*"There is really only one question:*
*Who am I?*
*There is really only one answer:*
*I am an extension of the mind of Creation*
*Experiencing itself in this dimension of perceived reality."*

P'Taah

If the Universe were likened to the ocean, teeming with existence, could we not be likened to drops of water from that ocean? Each drop would contain all of the ingredients present in this vast ocean of creation. We may visualize a teacup containing that drop of water from the ocean source, containing all that is within that source. The drop of ocean water may experience the free will to explore and leave its' home and chart a new adventure outside the "home" or source. This is done with the hope of experiencing an unknown existence and a unique adventure. Thus, the journey begins… the Spiritual Being is about to have a human experience.

The ocean, to many, represents a very special and sacred tie to our origins and the belief in the universal "Oneness." The belief is that the Oneness is contained in every drop of ocean water, regardless of what each drop may choose to experience in a physical existence. My own belief system stirred a dream for me that altered my thinking and attested to this metaphor of the ocean journey; the Oneness and the accompanying sadness of our separation from our source. At the time, I was in the throes of "empty-nesting" and letting-go of the last of my three children as they were leaving home and venturing onto their own new journeys. I thought I was doing well with the letting-go process, until I had a memorable and vivid dream, in which I found myself grieving as I strolled along a beautiful beach with the ocean spread before me. The mood was melancholy, until I began to see a brilliant white light rolling toward the shore. The white light had always, in my meditations, represented the presence of spirit. But this time, as it neared the shore, I became uneasy, because if I moved into that light, it would somehow mean I must say good-bye, and this, I did not feel ready to do. I resisted by digging my heels into the sand, until I suddenly saw a figure emerging in the bright light. It was my long deceased mother, dressed magnificently in her wedding dress of burgundy velvet, and long leather gloves, wearing an expression of great love and compassion. Resembling the Madonna as she hovered over the ocean, her magnificence was overwhelming. She extended her arms to me and as I instantly went to her, she held me and murmured, "there are no good-byes, we all are one."

The metaphysical symbolism here in the ocean, the white light, the wedding dress, and the loving countenance of the mother were all designed to assist in a transition to a higher level of understanding and awakening...the human journey moving into its greater level of development and transcendence.

The human mission as represented by the drop of sea water, now becomes a lesson in remembering our origins

and who we really are and why we left our source. The
journey becomes more complicated as the human
experience of physicality and lessons to be learned must
also involve an ego, which is fear-based, survival-based, and
primarily designed to keep us from remembering who we
really are…absolute perfection. During our life process, our
egos are our sensors of external life and our defenders
against perceived threats. However valuable they are, they
are not love-based. Their fear-based approach prevents the
extension of love, experimenting with new things, and most
of all, growing into the broad-based loving, balanced beings
we are all meant to be. Some fear-based people may choose
an ego defensive stance of power and control which may
have negative consequences. Life becomes very complex as
the ego develops and evolves, because now we have both
an interface with the physical life, complete with many
potential obstacles, and a higher spiritual essence and
existence to integrate into the human being. It becomes
invaluable to embrace a pathway of greater and greater
understanding, awakening and enlightenment. But first, we
must learn to navigate the passages of life and pass through
the many "stages" of our growth toward greater
enlightenment, free of fear. This growth can be depicted by
the pictorial representations of the change of seasons.
Here, many of our leaders and teachers such as Jesus,
Gandhi, Dali Lama and many others come immediately to
mind.

The Humanistic Psychologist, Abraham Maslow, seems
best to have captured the sequence of human
developmental issues in his *Hierarchy of Needs*. Maslow's
theory introduces the notion that people are moved to

action and reaction by needs that are both physical, as well as psychological. These needs are assembled in ascending order, from the most basic to the most lofty. The lower need must be reasonably met, before the next need can successfully be met. Most people have an impulse to improve themselves, an impulse toward actualizing more of their potentialities toward full humanness and human fulfillment. What then holds us back or blocks the full rise to our potential? This book will trace the implications of each level of development, the possible blocks, and then foster new coping skills in reaching for the ultimate goal of enlightenment and transcendence, i.e. remembering who we really are.

*But we must remember the four evolutionary principles of this new human existence:*

1) *The human purpose on Earth is to evolve physically, mentally, emotionally and spiritually.*
2) *Every human being has a Divine Essence made of light and love whose nature is goodness.*
3) *Free will is an absolute universal right; impeccability calls on the self to surrender its free will to Divine will with faith and trust.*
4) *All of natural existence is sacred beyond how it serves or meets the needs of the individual self.*

*As P'Taah states… "Your mission in life is simply to come to know who you really are."*

~

## Chapter 2- Maslow's Hierarchy of Needs

### <u>Stages of Human Development</u>

Healthy human development relies on early need gratification. Levels 1, 2, 3 (Basic physiological, Safety and Security, Love and Belonging), highlighted in green, are the needs most predominately met in the home by the primary caretakers. The primary caretakers are those who care for and nurture the infant, child, and adolescent, through young adulthood when the individual emancipates, i.e. college, military or living on their own. Physical and psychological growth must assist the child in discovering self-awareness. Most of us did not get these early needs met adequately enough to afford us easy sliding into adulthood. However, our "gifts of pain" always offer an opportunity to grow and change. Early unmet needs are not necessarily due to poor parenting, because most parents do the best they can. There could be many different reasons for lack of early need gratification, such as parents own lack of understanding, coping with their own difficulties, or fearing that there exists so many threats that they are unable to do anything, but survive.

The early stages, theoretically, should also foster a healthy sense of self, including individuation and a healthy sense of independence.

In viewing the innate characteristics with which the child is born (ten fingers, ten toes and senses to perceive the world around them), the child can thrive and grow and open new avenues of learning.

Ideally:

| GIVENS | + | SOCIALIZATION | = | EVOLVING HUMAN BEING |
|--------|---|---------------|---|----------------------|
| Sight | | Through communication, the child | | |
| Sound | | learns to interface with the outside world. | | |
| Smell | | Here the child can develop the means for | | |
| Taste | | getting his/her needs met, without | | |
| Touch | | intruding on another's process. | | |
| | | Essential here is self-awareness. | | |

The first three levels of Maslow's Hierarchy are the fundamentals of learning and becoming socialized into a family and a culture. It is important that a sound basis or springboard for moving out into the world be found in these early stages.  It is never too late to reclaim these early missed stages, perhaps through therapeutic intervention or availing oneself of relevant literature to study and change. Some factors in the early stages may be inborn or hereditarily active, such as family disorders, coping incapacities, physical ineptness or immaturity of primary caretakers, which need to be taken into consideration as the child matures. These beginning stages allow for the maturation of the ego, leading to an acceptance of what is realistic and reasonable. If problems develop in these early stages, i.e. lack of bonding, failure of boundaries, drug abuse in the family,  inability to separate and individuate properly, inherited anger issues, abuse and neglect, fear and coping inabilities, then the child may be forced "underground" and develop a "False" sense of identity in order to protect itself from vulnerabilities.  The "False" sense of self has an intention to protect, rather than to grow and learn.  The defenses that may be used are denial (refusal to accept reality), projection (blaming or putting own feelings on others), rationalization (excuses), and intellectualization (thinking, not feeling), to name a few. The "False" self (D.W. Winnicott) is defensive and closed to change or learning.  The "Real" self is open and able to learn.  The chart on the following page explains how the two identities compare:

| **"False" self (Protective Mode)** | **"Real" self (Learning Mode)** |
|---|---|
| Closed system | Open system |
| Fear-oriented | Love-oriented |
| Dysfunctional coping mechanisms | Creative/effective coping |
| Angry/blaming | Responsible |
| Controlling of others | Self-control |
| Victim role | Liberated role |
| Avoidant | Engaging |
| Holds on | Lets go |
| Judgmental | Accepting |
| Dependent | Independent |
| Passive/Aggressive | Assertive |
| Unwilling to grow | Desire to grow |

The "False" self leads to a protective mode of external, dysfunctional coping mechanisms, which will not readily allow for a healthy internal processing of growth-producing life management. The "False" self fills the void and covers the "Real" self with external methods of numbing, such as drugs, alcohol, criminal behavior, compulsive behavior, and codependency and mood disorders. When the "False" self takes over, the "Real" self becomes suppressed and cannot emotionally grow or learn or identify a healthy sense of self. Graphically, the "False" self dysfunctional evolutionary chart is as follows on the next page:

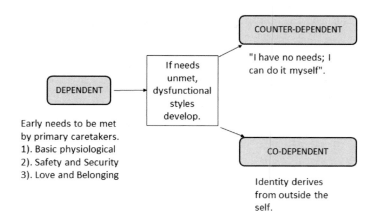

In the early dependent stage, the many needs of the child are physiological and psychological in nature. There is a need for responsive parenting, nurturance, role-modeling, imitating, limit-setting, boundary definition, loving, caring environment, and cooperation between the primary care givers, to mention a few of the needs. As often happens, there can be many loopholes in the very difficult task of child rearing. Generally, if there are issues in childhood, they can be part of one or/both categories of dysfunction. Codependency and counter dependency, as delineated by Selma Fraiberg, can stem from early inadequacies in the child's ability to develop a healthy sense of self. Codependency, in today's world, is a much overused statement, but its meaning is simply, deriving more of one's identity from outside sources, than from inside the self. These outside sources can be anything from money, work, social activity, a person or love interest to career or any attention-seeking source. What becomes sacrificed here is the internal sense of self. Codependency is a set of maladaptive, compulsive behaviors learned in a family where surviving emotional stress or pain is paramount.

Characteristics of codependency: low self-esteem, fear of rejection, fear of not being good enough, addiction to outside sources of validation, perfectionism, boundary impairment, shame, difficulty owning one's own reality, difficulty taking care of self, preoccupation with pleasing and caring for others, operating in the extremes, self-judgment, self-persecution and the need to be needed. Counter dependency is withdrawal from everyone and everything, especially those who are not attending to or meeting the individual's needs. Statements such as "I need no one; I have no needs; I can do it myself." Usually, this is the result of anger directed at a perceived environment that is un-giving, unaccepting or unavailable, over which the individual has no control. Therefore, withdrawal is the only escape.

Remedies for these behaviors, often in a therapeutic setting, begin with verbalizing one's own reality, taking responsibility for feelings, especially shame without blaming, assessing boundaries, and establishing healthy new ones, i.e. ability to say "No", beginning to esteem from within, responding with moderation, taking care of own needs and wants, and learning assertiveness. This may require some outside help from a professional, who can assist in accessing the suppressed "Real" self. The "Real" self must learn the new tool of detaching with love, which means mentally, emotionally, and physically disengaging from unhealthy and painful entanglements with another person's life and responsibilities, and from problems we can't solve. A helpful tool here is a poem entitled, *Comes the Dawn* by Kara Degiovanna:

*"After a while you learn*
*the subtle difference*
*between holding a hand*
*and chaining a soul.*
*And you learn*
*that love doesn't mean leaning*
*and company doesn't mean security.*
*And you begin to learn*
*that kisses aren't contracts*
*and presents aren't promises.*
*And you begin to accept your defeats*
*with your head up and your eyes ahead*
*with the grace of a woman or a man*
*not the grief of a child,*
*and you learn to build all your roads on today*
*because tomorrow's ground is*
*too uncertain for plans*
*and futures have a way of falling down*
*in midflight.*
*After a while you learn*
*that even sunshine burns if you ask too much.*
*So you plant your own garden*
*And decorate your own soul*
*instead of waiting for someone to bring you flowers.*
*And you learn*
*that you really can endure*
*that you really do have worth.*
*And you learn*
*And you learn*
*with every goodbye, you learn…"*

~

MARILYN BROOKHART

## Chapter 3- Relationship Implications

Before beginning to examine the implications of personal dysfunction in regard to relationships, Virginia Satir in 1976 outlined some personal tools to remember when reaching for a new way of relating to the world around us.

*"To See and Hear*
*what is here,*
*Instead of what should be, was or will be.*
*To Say what one feels and thinks,*
*Instead of what one should.*
*To Feel what one feels,*
*Instead of what one ought.*
*To Ask for what one wants,*
*Instead of always waiting for permission*
*To Take Risks in one's own behalf,*
*Instead of choosing to be "secure" and not rocking the boat."*

In relationships with the typical use of "False" self coping mechanisms (codependent and/or counter dependent), the relationship becomes very difficult, very unfulfilling and in many cases impossible to sustain. The "False" self is not the true self, but a cover for an insecure and uncertain sense of self. The true self may emerge when angry or faced with insurmountable challenges. In relationships, this can cause immense stress and pressure on the relationship. Current divorce statistics demonstrate this... Over 50% of marriages end in divorce in the U.S.

## "False" self COPING MECHANISMS;

Codependency

1) Enmeshment
2) No healthy independent "Me's" visible
3) Only identity is "We"
4) No boundaries
5) Fear of abandonment
6) Caretaker of other's needs

Counter Dependency

1) Two frustrated and angry "Me's"
2) Walls, instead of boundaries
3) Inability to be vulnerable
4) Fear of exposure
5) Thin thread holds the "Me's" together

## "Real" self COPING MECHANISMS;

Assertive

1) Two healthy, functional and independent "Me's"
2) Participate in nurturing each other's growth
3) Respectful of self and others.
4) Mature
5) Supportive

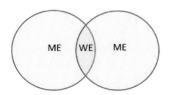

Relationships can be very difficult, if either or both individuals are needing the other to adequately define them, as they would like to be seen. Without understanding and evaluating the dysfunctional "False" self with its faulty coping mechanisms, neither person can disentangle from the web of co or counter dependency. Repetition of old patterns will continue to keep the person locked in a cycle of "insanity." As the phrase goes… "The definition of insanity is repeating the same behaviors expecting different results." Change can never happen. Therein lies the Rub!

The "False" self attempts to maneuver or coerce certain behaviors from the environment. In other words, the "False" self cannot deal with "Real" or perceived abandonment, so it will do almost anything to hold onto and control the other person, who represents a major part of them. Accessing the "Real" self may not be possible until some personal, insight-oriented work on self-awareness has a chance to help with impaired identity.

Each person involved in any type of relationship or interaction with another, for it to be reasonably successful, must understand past, present and future motivations. For example:
A little girl growing up in a family with an alcoholic father, may very well have a tendency to marry an alcoholic husband. There are two reasons for this. Firstly, she is accustomed to dealing with an alcoholic person and either she may be an enabler or a very angry person, out to change everything. Secondly, if she is successful in changing her husband, it may represent, to her "inner" child, success at finally changing her father into an available parent. Husband becomes a stand-in for the absent father.

The "False" self utilizes many defenses, but probably the most persistent one is control. As mentioned previously, the "False" self must, for their own preservation, take charge of others in as many different ways as possible. Otherwise, feelings of abandonment and rejection ensue, leading to depression and anxiety.

The *Big Book of Alcoholics Anonymous*, a very enlightened and astute informational outlet, offers many recovering individuals an understanding of the process of evolving to a higher level.

The following is a modified excerpt from this Big Book:

> *"And acceptance is the answer to all my problems today. When I am disturbed, it is because I find some person, place, thing or situation; some fact of my life unacceptable to me, and I can find no serenity until I accept that person, place, thing or situation as being exactly the way it is supposed to be at this moment. Nothing, absolutely nothing, happens in God's world by mistake. Unless I accept life completely on life's terms, I cannot be happy. I need to concentrate not so much on what needs to be changed in the world, as on what needs to be changed in me and in my attitudes."*

~

Spring

## Chapter 4- Inner Child Work

The Inner Child Work is often called "original pain work", designed to remember what did or didn't happen as the child navigated the difficult path of growing up. It is the most basic, comprehensive and effective method for the "working through" process of our earliest developmental encounters with unpleasant or painful experiences from childhood. All humans by nature experience some wounds, either major or minor, especially from our earlier years when there was little or no control. Much of this pain has been sublimated or buried deeply within the unconscious mind. Some is easily accessible, but that which is buried deeply is recognized only as dysfunctional adult manifestations.

One pioneer in the understanding of human psychosocial stages of development is Erik Erikson. He delineated eight stages in which the child must resolve conflicts in the first four stages, in order to move into the last four stages as an adult. Few master these first four with grace and ease. The stages are as follows:

1) Trust vs Mistrust - (first year of life) Environment must be orderly and predictable. Also, found in Maslow's second level of Safety and Security.
2) Autonomy vs Doubt - (2 and 3 years) Develop motor and mental abilities, as well as have opportunities to explore and manipulate environment within a safe, child-proof structure.
3) Initiative vs Guilt - (4 and 5 years) Positive response to self-initiated activities, mental or physical.
4) Industry vs Inferiority - (6-11 years) Curiosity in learning how things work and learning to formulate rules, organize order and attend to it industriously.
5) Identity vs Role Confusion - (12-18 years) Develop multiple ways of perceiving, recognizing other's points

of view, behaving differently in different situations, and adaptability. The identity is one's own and distinct from all others, not just a mirror of the parents.

6) Intimacy vs Isolation - (young adulthood, 16-25 years.) Ability to reach out and make contact with others; ability to form intimate relationships, sexually, emotionally and morally. Also, the ability to sustain close personal relationships with different types of people.

7) Generativity vs Self-Absorption - (later-adulthood, 25-40 years). Concerned with passing on to future generations, the knowledge, skills and information gathered during one's lifetime.

8) Integrity vs Despair - (elder years) One can enjoy the fulfillment of one's life with a sense of integrity.

The first four stages are concerned with the child's development and the last four, with the adult's development. Each is critical to the mastery of the next stage, just as in Maslow's stages of human development. Trust, Autonomy, Initiative, and Industry, tasks for the child to "master" are quite frequently underdeveloped or one or more missed completely. The task for the adult must be to go back and reclaim these missed growth opportunities.

John Bradshaw, seemingly the Father of Inner Child Work, wrote a book, entitled *Homecoming, Reclaiming and Championing Your Inner Child*. This meaningful, experiential book, works on each stage of a child's life, from infancy to young adulthood, with hands-on exercises for the reader to do. He begins with questions, pointed at the particular stage and corresponding to what should have been accomplished, many of which were not. For example; Questions for the Toddler age group might be, "Do you have trouble knowing what you want?"

or "Do you have great fears of abandonment?" or "Do you find yourself in frequent conflicts with people in authority?" Answering "yes" to any of these may be a signal that current presenting issues relate back to the toddler stage. There are generally 20-25 questions in each stage. In addition to the questions usable in diagnosing, there are healing affirmations that can be put into a recording for one's own healing and relaxation. Examples of Infant affirmations include… "Welcome to the world, I've been waiting for you", or "I like you just the way you are", or "In all the world, there has never been another like you." These questions and affirmations are also coupled with a written debriefing of all that can be remembered from each stage and letters written to and from the wounded inner child.

In my practice, I used this book with a long-standing alcohol recovery group that had been together for many years. I asked, for those who wanted to participate, if they would purchase a baby doll that resembled them, and for one week, take this doll with them everywhere they went. They all chose to do this in a meaningful, yet playful manner and enjoyed the exercise. It seemed to make the inner child very "Real" and brought the exercise to life. One gentleman bought himself a Raggedy Andy doll, which had been his constant companion as a child, and he took it everywhere he went. He reported to the group, a very funny experience he had when he made a visit to the hospital to visit a friend. He took Andy with him into the hospital and a nurse happened to catch a glimpse and said as she passed, "Inner Child?" In the 90's, Inner Child Work was a popular therapeutic devise and presumably, not that strange a sight.

Each of Bradshaw's stages of development, with its questions and healing affirmations are attempts to rework the perceptions of childhood into a healing mode and a manageable understanding of each person's history so it will no longer hold the person prisoner. The very wise saying, "It's never too late to have a happy childhood" can be absolutely true. We change the perception; we change the feeling and viewpoint, without defenses, such as avoidance, or denial. We've taken charge of our lives.

People from dysfunctional families were probably parented by wounded adults. They learned the "Don't talk", "Don't trust", "Don't feel" rules. They also, learned to blame themselves, feel alone, seek approval and attention, feel powerless and hopeless and have no idea why or how this happened. Bradshaw sites six steps necessary to heal the wounded inner child. They are:

1) **Trust** - need a supportive, non-judgmental person to hear and validate their story.
2) **Validate** - the wounds, shame, abuse, neglect and caretaking that the child had to do.
3) **Shock and anger** - feel the anger about experiencing the exposure to life-challenging consequences.
4) **Sadness** - at being betrayed, victimized and experiencing a loss of positive dreams.
5) **Remorse** - regarding the childhood abandonment, over which he/she had no control.
6) **Loneliness** - the toxic shame of parental abandonment leads to feelings of loneliness.

The objective here is to return to childhood as an adult and heal the deep wounds and pains.
We have an innate and natural ability to heal our own pain.

A useful meditative, visualization for the inner child is as follows:

- Visualize your inner child (age 4) playing quietly in the front yard of the home, where you lived at that age.
- The adult "you" approaches your child and speaking very gently and quietly, asks the child to accompany you.
- You both walk hand in hand down to the end of the street.
- Before you turn the corner, both of you turn around and see your parents standing in the front yard.
- You both wave "good-bye" to them and continue on around the corner.
- Once around the corner, your most trusted friend is there waiting for you both.
- Pick up your little child and cuddle and love them, then momentarily turn him/her over to the most trusted friend, who does the same. The friend then turns the child back to you to be shrunk and put back inside you.
- If the child will not accompany you around the corner, let them go back to the parents. However, make a date to come back the next day and help the child to try it again.

This is a very sensitive, and for some, extremely difficult exercise in remembering and working through the wounds of childhood. It's probably not for everyone, but it is a very effective tool, for those wanting, once and for all, to be free of the old bonds that have kept them from achieving their highest potential.

~

MARILYN BROOKHART

## Chapter 5- Separation/Individuation

In lay terms, separation/individuation simply means the child being enabled to move into an individuated sense of self. But this, by no means, is a simple or uncomplicated task, because of the many unforeseen things that may or may not happen. The child must "cut the cord' or "cut the apron strings" so to speak and begin to develop his/her own sense of identity, as different from the primary caretakers. The fundamental stages of separation/individuation involve:

1) Infant moving from a symbiotic (merged with the mother) relationship to...
2) Mother figure as a need-gratifier to...
3) Mother figure valued for her functionality to...
4) Mother as a loving figure regardless of need.

This progression allows the child to move successfully into his/her own identity and a rudimentary sense of his/her own autonomy. If this is a successful transition, the child hopefully will be free of dependency defenses, as discussed in Chapter 2, idealizations, insecurities, degradations, neediness, codependences, emptiness, deep fears, phobias, and anger, outside the normal "growing pains."
In Althea Horner's study of human development, she explains how the child moves from stage to stage beginning at birth to 3 years of age, when a reasonable identity has begun to emerge. In the beginning, the infant must form an attachment to the primary caretaker(s). Though the intense attachment or symbiosis (merged with mother; no discernment between mother and self) must dissolve into

the development of one's own identity, there are necessary stages that the child and primary caretaker must successfully navigate before the achievement of the self-identity goal.

This first stage of <u>symbiosis</u> or attachment gives way to the second stage, at 4-5 months, which is <u>differentiation.</u> Here, the child deciphers that mother or primary caretaker is different from him/her. Mother is separate and sometimes out of sight for short or long periods of time. The mother functions as a point of reference, a framework for the individuating child. This can be the beginning of "stranger anxiety." Too many different faces may cause some anxiety for the child, who is busy trying to understand the function of mother and then a "strange face" and what it means to them. The next stage, at about 10 to 16 months, is <u>practicing</u>. The child is now advancing rapidly, in terms of locomotion (creeping, crawling and walking) and the ability to explore and learn. The child is beginning to perceive and learn about the world around him/her and trying to make some sense of how it all operates. This is the start of the "No" and the "Don't touch" world. The culmination of this practicing stage at mid second year brings the child's belief system to the point of all "powerful magic." This derives from the sense of sharing in mother's "magical powers." (Mahler; 1968).

At approximately 18 months, the next critical step in the separation/individuation process is the <u>rapprochement</u> stage. Here the toddler becomes more aware of his separation from the mother figure and wants to venture out on his/her own explorations, but needs to know that mother is still somewhere close by, so he/she can come running back, if necessary to check in. This is important for the child to develop a sense of safety and security, even if he/she cannot see or experience her at the moment, she or a surrogate will be returning to reenter his/her world. This is called "object constancy" or the ability to retain the image of the returning caretaker; that he/she has not been abandoned. The child, on an unconscious level, trusts that mother or a surrogate will be returning to be with him/her the way she was earlier. Object is anyone outside the individual and constancy is the ability to continue to perceive that object, despite the fact that they are not currently present in the individuals' environment or line of vision. This is of obvious importance, in light of the frequent use of day care or preschool, where the child is away from mother for periods of time. The peek-a-boo game as played by mother and baby is an example of how difficult it is for the young baby to not be able to see and respond to the mother figure. When the mother stands over the baby and coos and talks to him/her and they smile with delight, but then she puts a handkerchief over her face, the baby is frightened and begins to cry. But when mother drops the handkerchief, the baby smiles again. By the age of 3 the child should have, at least, attained a rudimentary sense of self and a trust that mother/father, grandparent, nanny or sibling will be there for the child. When it is age appropriate, the child will become more and more independent and loosen the need to have someone omnipresent.

There are some clinical issues that may develop during this separation/individuation stage, but for the most part, children are able to navigate this developmental level with only minor difficulty. The parents, however, may have their own difficulties in letting go, as it is age appropriate. Some adults and children can experience issues that may trace their origins to the various areas of separation/individuation. Difficulties here can result in lack of achievement, emotional imbalance, social maladjustment, rejection, inconsistency or overly demanding. The individual may develop fears or phobias regarding risk-taking, change, or thinking "out of the box." But these are issues, barring any chemical deficiency that can be addressed at any point in a person's life, if they feel a need to change.

The child may get many different chances to navigate the separation/individuation phase of life…childhood, teen years, adulthood or not at all. For the young child, it will be the "no" or "I can do it myself" stage or the rebellious teen, experimenting with their own different or unusual appearance and actions. A personal example of this would be when, one morning, my teenage daughter came downstairs for breakfast and was wearing one of my sweaters. I mentioned this to her and her response was, "I know, and I hate it, but I have nothing else to wear." She had to make it clear that any part or hint of "me" was to be excluded from her equation. Some people can grow to adulthood and still have many issues with attachment, neediness, or clinginess, such as one sees in codependency and enmeshment or marrying a partner who very closely resembles a parent with whom he/she had the most difficulty in finding approval or in being validated. Or there are those who move far away from the family of origin in order to geographically relocate in order to believe on some level that they have successfully separated and individuated from their family. Rarely do any of these pseudo-operating tools achieve success, because separation/individuation is a psychological process, not a physical one.

To summarize life's evolving conditions and necessary tasks to be overcome; I refer to M. Scott Peck's, *The Road Less Traveled*, 1978. The following conditions must be released in order to live a whole and successful life:

*"The state of infancy, in which no external demands need to be heeded.*
*The fantasy of omnipotence.*
*The desire for total possession of one's parent(s).*
*The dependency of childhood.*
*Distorted images of one's parents.*
*The Omni potentiality of adolescence.*
*The freedom of non- commitment*
*The agility of youth.*
*The sexual attractiveness and/ or potency of youth.*
*The fantasy of immortality.*
*Authority over one's children.*
*Various forms of temporal power.*
*The independence of physical health.*
*And, ultimately the self and life itself."*

These are growth-producing processes, but only to an open mind that is willing to look within, explore and acknowledge one's own shortcomings. This self-knowledge must be used to make the necessary changes that will enable one to reach higher levels in Maslow's *Hierarchy of Needs*, i.e. self-esteem, self-actualization and transcendence.

~

## Chapter 6- Sense of Self and Self-Esteem

In understanding separation/individuation, we must know that it is a necessary part and the next stage of becoming the autonomous person of high integrity that we wish to be. Experiencing a healthy separation/individuation enables us to bypass the codependent/counter dependent defenses and move into a state of independency and autonomy. If we remain codependent, we are probably more invested in someone else's life, than our own. In CODA, Codependents Anonymous, there is a long-standing joke... "A codependent had a near death experience and saw someone else's life pass before them." One of the most significant attributes of codependency is "Caretaking" of others. Caretaking is doing for others what they can do for themselves. This Caretaking does not allow a person to try their wings and learn how to fly on their own or to make their own decisions. We, then, are taking away their life lessons and doing it for them. Caretaking is often referred to as "Enabling." This is why caretaking with a drug/alcohol addicted person does not give them the opportunity to make decisions based on what they think is in their best interest. This is why they often fail at a recovery program, because they had not reached the decision on their own. Al-Anon, the recovery group for the loved ones of the alcoholic teaches "Detaching with love." It's easy to detach with anger and this is where huge fights ensue and the codependents throw the bottles out, threaten divorce, fight and challenge the alcoholic, but the alcoholic puts all of his or her energy into fighting this off, instead of facing their addiction, holding him/herself accountable and going into recovery. They may need to be allowed to hit "their bottom", but they can't when someone else is taking responsibility for their illness.

Instead of "Caretaking", we can learn to become "Caregivers" or supporters of the other person's highest level of functioning. Stephen Paul writes "To be free yourself, you have to release everyone else." Furthermore, they must feel confident enough to welcome the release, so they can grow and learn self-sufficiency.

The new diagram below continues to expand on this dependency theme to help move into independency, and then into interdependence. This I call the Evolutionary Cycle.

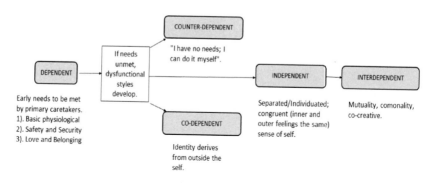

There are many obstacles that can interfere with the complicated process of separation/individuation and object constancy, resulting in incomplete emancipation. These problems include such things as trying to control and/or possess the other person, insatiable desire to keep doing for others, a narcissistic (external admiration) need to be perfect in the eyes of the public, insatiable compulsion to put all others, before one's self, to the point of neglecting themselves. These all lead to a sense of neediness, emptiness and lack, codependency and caretaking. These can be major issues for people in the healing professions, i.e. doctor, nurses, all types of therapists (physical, mental, energy, occupational, speech). Many in the psychotherapeutic community have entered this field, without having worked through their own issues, in other words "have not done their work." With many of their own issues unresolved, they are apt to be more caretakers or do-gooders. They can contaminate the client's therapy, by taking their lessons away or by jumping in and unconsciously trying to resolve their own issues, as well as the client's. They may also steer the client away from issues they don't understand or wish to deal. This is a threat to the client because, at best, they never truly work on their issues and at worst; the therapist does it for them, i.e. unproductive caretaking. A popular saying in *Al-Anon*, the 12 step counter-part of AA, composed of loved ones of the alcoholic, states...God never closes one door, without opening another, but it sure is hell in the hallway. The statement is indicative of the hard work that lies ahead, in the form of confronting their inner turmoil and dealing with the change. This can be the most difficult part of the journey, because it requires desire and perseverance in changing old patterns. Young people, especially, have a hard time being vulnerable and laying their omnipotence aside. Lack of vulnerability is the major problem in undertaking any new change or growth in order to become the person he or she would want to be. The guilt-ridden "shoulds" of life are also pitfalls that keep us locked into a lack of helpful changes that improve our sense of self. My philosophy is, if you can't change the "should" into a "want-to", then don't do it. It's hard to own a "should", but not a "want-to." There once was a popular t-shirt that read… Don't "Should" on me! It says it all about setting appropriate limits.

Goethe states that "self-love and self-esteem come from trusting the self to know how to live. The person who does not love him/her self is out of balance." This lack involves issues with humility, character, hidden agendas and integrity. Integrity is what we do when no one is looking. Another important issue in the separation/individuation process is learning detachment with love, which means mentally, emotionally, and physically disengaging ourselves from unhealthy and painful entanglements with another person's life and responsibilities, and from problems we can't solve.

In looking at the psychotherapist's issues, I'd like to site an example of visible evidence of how other peoples' worlds can enter the therapist's world, unseen and unnoticed. In my early days of practice, and although I had done considerable "work on myself", it was always possible to discover a new wrinkle that needed to be addressed. Because of my interest in new world thought and spiritual philosophies, I heartily pursued metaphysical conferences, body and soul conferences, channelings, peace missions abroad, EarthWatch trips to various parts of the world, aura and energy healings, and studies in The *Course in Miracles*, all designed to broaden my knowledge of new non-mainstream material. In my pursuits, I discovered a devise, called a Q-Link that is a necklace worn around the neck that purports to activate a protective field around the body and cleanse the aura, the energy field around every person. The Q-Link, because of its copper tubing has the capacity to help prevent or diminish an excess of electrical activity in the brain. Electromagnetic energy or fields are well known in the scientific world of electronics and their effects on humans. The Q-Link has been shown to mitigate effects of electromagnetic fields (EMF's) on EEG patterns. There are now special cameras, called Cerulean cameras that can measure the energy fields in one's aura and gauge the various energies of the person being photographed, by the colors that appear around the upper body. The camera is connected to a high voltage source, and thus is able to produce an image on a photographic plate. To date, my aura photographs have consisted, primarily of blues and greens, indicating relative peace and harmony. An occasional red makes an appearance, which can be indicative of too much stress.

Some time ago, in the early days of practice, I attended a Body and Soul Conference. There was a Q-link booth there that was using a Cerulean camera to photograph fingertip pictures, when using the Q-link. I began a discussion with the attendants at the booth and told them that I owned a Q-link, but had not worn it for a while. She asked if we could do an experiment in which they would photograph my fingertips today for a "before" picture, wear the Q-link overnight and return the next day for an "after" picture. I readily agreed because it sounded interesting. The "before" picture revealed many tiny, little filament or tentacles coming off my fingertips. They immediately asked if I were a nurse or doctor; I said I was a psychotherapist, to which they replied, "of course you are." The filaments represent outside forces in my aura. It was obvious to them that I worked extensively with people, in some capacity. I did as I was instructed, to wear the Q-Link overnight, and when I returned the next day for my "after" picture, it was almost startling. My fingertip photograph revealed very little, if any, filaments protruding from my fingers. The Q-Link had managed to clear much of the extra, outside energy from my aura. But here also, was evidence that in the healing professions especially, we are not always aware of how much extra outside "stuff" we take on. This, in itself, could cause early burnout.

In summary, the issues of codependency, counter dependency, incongruency, lack of object constancy, caretaking, unresolved anger, unhealthy self-medicating, and narcissistic concerns with self, are all unsatisfying modes of living and learning. They preclude the development of a genuine sense of self-esteem, with its accompanying sense of peace and harmony.

~

Summer

MARILYN BROOKHART

## Chapter 7- Addictive and Compulsive Disorders

An addictive disorder may be another stumbling block along life's journey, but fortunately they are all treatable. Addictive disorders can run the gamut from substance abuse to overeating, to gambling, to addictive relationships, to even compulsive shoplifting. By definition, an addictive disorder is a habitual need to repeat certain behaviors, knowing they're not in the person's best interest. Any addiction can be classified as a disease, because it has the capacity to change the brain chemistry and become physiological in body functioning and in brain constitution and activity. The EEG of an addictive person, before and after, changes dramatically, meaning the brain becomes markedly different than it was before the addictive process took control of the individual. Particularly in alcoholism, so prevalent in western cultures, many physiological and neurological symptoms occur that cannot be accounted for by a "moral" failure or dysfunction. Unfortunately, these brain changes and damages can be transmitted to future generations, giving substance abuse a genetic component.

In looking at the brain's reaction to an overload of alcohol, I'll use an analogy of a light bulb (brain), a battery (brain's electrical system) and the maintenance of homeostasis (balance).

A battery is hooked up to a light bulb, and the bulb shines brightly with the battery's current, until a resistor enters the mix. The resistor stops the flow of electrical current, so another battery needs to be added to maintain balance. Alcohol is the resistor, and the more alcohol ingested, the more batteries need to be employed to maintain the brain's balance of electricity. This leads to too much electrical activity in the brain, and becomes a major overload for the brain to handle. The brain needs homeostasis, and so keeps adding "juice", so that balance is maintained. If the drinking suddenly stops, there is an enormous abundance of electrical brain activity, which can cause everything to short-out. The brain's chemistry goes wild. At best, a hangover ensues, at worst, the DT's (Delirium Tremors) or seizures can incapacitate the individual. This is the same thing experienced by a schizophrenic with brain activity and impulses out of control and the whole system is on overload.

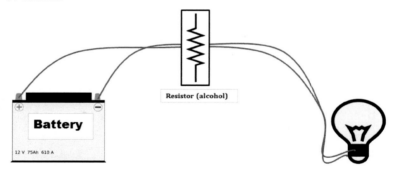

Some generalized symptoms of the progression of the disease of alcoholism are as follows;

<u>Early Warning Signs</u>
1) Relief drinking.
2) Increased tolerance ( takes more alcohol to get the same effect).
3) Preoccupation with alcohol.
4) Reluctance to discuss drinking.
5) Surreptitious (secret) drinking.

### Prodromal (early) Stage
1) Increased relief drinking.
2) Surreptitious drinking.
3) Preoccupation with alcohol.
4) Onset of alcohol related problems.
5) Memory lapses/blackouts.
6) Periods of self-enforced abstinence.

### Mid Stage
1) Continuous relief drinking.
2) Increased tolerance.
3) Continuous alcohol related problems.
4) Feelings of guilt and remorse.

### Late Stage
1) Tolerance decreases.
2) Hopelessness/despair.
3) Physical debilitation.
4) Spiritual exhaustion (loss of faith in anything of higher value).
5) Out-of-touch with reality.

### Custodial Care Stage
1) Life sustained by monitored dosages of alcohol.

Because substance or any other addiction is a family disease, all members have specific and very rigid roles to play in this whole family system, in order to maintain even dysfunctional homeostasis. The difference between a functional and a dysfunctional family is, in the functional family, the parents are there to meet the needs of the children; in a dysfunctional family, the children are groomed to meet the needs of the parents. And so the dysfunctional family must decipher how to maintain homeostasis and balance with an abundance of dysfunction surrounding them.

The following diagram may explain the family constellation and the necessary roles to be played in the family. These roles are adhered to rigidly, in order to maintain some semblance of balance.

These roles are also relevant in any family, but the difference is, in functional families these roles are fluid, flexible and not aimed at protecting the dysfunctionality of the family secrets and they may switch to different family members or within one specific person.

| ROLES | VISIBLE QUALITIES | INNER FEELINGS | REPRESENTAION TO THE FAMILY |
|---|---|---|---|
| Family Hero | Receives positive attention<br>High achiever<br>Visible success<br>Does what's right | Inadequate<br>Inferior<br>Guilty<br>Some narcissism | Family's self-worth<br>Structure<br>Stability<br>Family pride |
| Scape Goat | Receives negative attention<br>Hostility<br>Defiance<br>Anger<br>Acts out | Hurt<br>Guilt<br>Abandonment | Deflects focus away from the<br>dysfunctionality<br>"Squeaky Wheel" gets the<br>negative attention |
| Lost Child | Withdrawn<br>Loner<br>Follower<br>Trouble making decisions<br>Invisible | Loneliness<br>Powerlessness<br>Unimportant<br>Suicidal<br>Depressed | Relief<br>One child family doesn't have to<br>worry about |
| Mascot/Clown | Fragile<br>Immature<br>Joker<br>Hyperactive<br>Learning disabled | Fear<br>Anxiety<br>Stressed | Comic relief<br>Fun and humor<br>Lightens load |

*(For enlarged image of this diagram go to page 87)*

The greatest disturbance or imbalance in any of these roles is the hidden anger. If we have any societal fault, it is hiding our own anger from ourselves. Anger generally hides the fear of not being good enough, being violated, or not being able to compete in our highly competitive society. If hidden and misunderstood, anger can undermine or even destroy the chosen pathway in life. It can, of course, push one into self-medicating to dull the anger and rage. There are really only two feelings we can have...love and fear, with each having their own sub categories. Anger always covers fear in some form. An easy test of our feelings at any given moment could be, "Am I extending love, even if I'm setting appropriate limits, or am I crying out for love." An example of extending love is an approach of amiability, cordiality and inclusiveness of all people, regardless of whom or what they are. They also spread positivity wherever they go. An example of crying out for love would be constant complaining, nagging, criticizing others, angering and spreading negativity wherever they go. If we're honest, we will be able to take charge of our situation, without controlling the other person and consider making necessary changes for the better.

The following is a checklist for hidden anger that may be helpful in our self-examination. Check each item that applies:

- ____Procrastination in the completion of imposed tasks.
- ____Perpetual or habitual lateness.
- ____A liking for sadistic or ironic humor.
- ____Sarcasm, cynicism or flippancy in conversation.
- ____Over politeness, constant cheerfulness, attitude of "grin and bear it."
- ____Frequent sighing.

- ____Smiling while hurting.
- ____Frequent disturbing or frightening dreams.
- ____Over-controlled monotone speaking voice.
- ____Boredom, apathy, loss of interest in things about which one would ordinarily be enthusiastic.
- ____Difficulty in getting to sleep or sleeping through the night.
- ____Slowing down of movements.
- ____Getting tired more easily than usual.
- ____Excessive irritability over trifles.
- ____Getting drowsy at inappropriate times.
- ____Sleeping more than usual (12-14 hours).
- ____Waking up tired, rather than rested or refreshed.
- ____Clenched jaw, especially while sleeping.
- ____Facial tics, spasmodic foot movements, habitual fist clenching, and similar repeated acts, done unintentionally or without awareness.
- ____Grinding teeth, especially while sleeping.
- ____Chronically stiff or sore neck or shoulder muscles.
- ____Stomach ulcers.
- ____Disease (dis-ease).

If these symptoms sound similar to anxiety and/or depression, they are. Much of anxiety, depression and anger appear together and come from the same stressful source...Fear!

Many people are totally unaware of how much suppression of negative feelings they manage on a daily basis. We have been taught that anger and negativity are undesirable and should not be openly expressed. Yet, within our culture, we are currently living in one of the most randomly violent periods in our history, without being at war. It would appear that anger and hostility either get "stuffed" or are acted-out in unhealthy and unproductive ways. Nonaggressive tools are a "**must**" in learning to interact in a helpful and productive way.

The following chapter will discuss our psychological needs, ways we choose to meet those needs and productive tools that will help to tame that negativity.

~

## Chapter 8- Body/Mind Connection

I begin this chapter with a short story by Portia Nelson:
*An Autobiography in Five Short Chapters*

### I.

*"I walk down the street.*
*There is a deep hole in the sidewalk*
*I fall in*
*I am lost...I am helpless*
               *It isn't my fault.*
*It takes forever to find a way out.*

### II.

*I walk down the same street.*
*There is a deep hole in the sidewalk*
*I pretend I don't see it.*
*I fall in again.*
*I can't believe I am in the same place,*
               *but it isn't my fault.*
*It still takes a long time to get out.*

### III.

*I walk down the same street.*
*There is a deep hole in the sidewalk.*
*I see it is there.*
*I still fall in...it's a habit.*
*My eyes are open.*
*I know where I am. It is my fault.*
*I get out immediately.*

IV.
*I walk down the same street*
*There is a deep hole in the sidewalk*
*I walk around it.*


V.
*I walk down another street."*


The basic understanding of this story is, if the mental process is dysfunctional and repeats habitual thinking, then the body follows with its dysfunctional reaction. Recalling the definition of "insanity"...repeating behaviors, expecting different results. It keeps us locked in. The mind adheres to one thought process and as long as it remains the same, the behavior remains the same. We need to be mindful and allow ourselves to "change our mind", and then the body is free to follow a new course. This story says it all, in terms of our growth from any form of dysfunctionality to a space of awareness, peace, harmony and mindfulness. How do we move ourselves forward and embrace the love and light that surrounds us? It does seem to take a lot of understanding and awareness to be a human at this time on this planet. But aware we must be, if we are going to understand, from our highest vantage point, the purpose of this human journey.

Bernie Siegel, M.D. did extensive research on the mind/body connection. In his best-selling book, *Love, Medicine and Miracles*, he cites his work with terminally ill children, utilizing visualization to help in their recoveries. His success rate in remissions was extremely noteworthy. *Love, Medicine and Miracles*, is a remarkable study in self-healing, as an adjunct to the medical model. In utilizing all of our options, we bring into play, not only the medical profession, with its advanced knowledge base, but all the alternative methods, old "folk medicine", as well as psychic override. The list is endless...acupuncture, meditation, yoga, energy healing, "body talk", medical intuition, aromatherapy, visualization, hypnotherapy, past life regression, rebirthing, Native American healing, and many more, all designed to mobilize our own innate healing abilities.

Woody Allen used to say that human beings are divided into mind and body: the mind embraces all of the nobler aspirations, like poetry and philosophy, but the body has all the fun. His movies frequently reflect that belief system.

My belief involves more of a systemic process with enormous connections that join the body, mind and spirit in one intercommunicative, cooperating system. Its purpose is to take impeccable care of what we enjoy and the mechanism that propels us forward in our growth. Louise Hay states, "We need to have a positive mental attitude about ourselves and about life." She also feels we need to have a strong spiritual connection. "When these three things are balanced, we rejoice in living." This means choosing to take part in our own healing process. Louise Hay has written much on the metaphysical understanding of physical illness. Psychologists, too, have shown that the effects of love on the body can now be measured: An unloved infant will have retarded bone growth and may even die; a stroked and loved infant grows faster and healthier. People who meditate and journal were shown to have enhanced immune systems. Love and peace of mind do truly protect us, and help us survive peacefully, as well as confront our pain and suffering with relative ease. Pain may also help us to interpret our symptoms and use them as motivators and redirectors. This has been seen with many heart attack victims, who completely turn their lives around and embrace a totally new and healthier way of life. Our "gift of pain" is often our greatest gift of healing and surviving in a sometimes difficult world environment. Our mental thought patterns may contribute greatly to the way we experience life. Doctors who remain open and willing to understand and utilize all options for helping their patients to heal are generally the busiest and most beloved by their patients. This is today's "holistic healing."

I had my own success in treating an eight year old boy with Tourette's syndrome, a nervous system disorder, involving involuntary repetitious movements or vocalizations, i.e. tics, jerking muscle spasms, and constant movements, primarily facial. I used guided imagery and visualization to calm his nervous system to the point where his tics subsided substantially. Soon, he became able to integrate his own calming tools, and ultimately, he became symptom free. Biofeedback became the tool of choice to maintain his level of relaxation and calm. Biofeedback releases the parts of the brain that get stuck or frozen and helps the brain to reorganize and relax so it can heal naturally.

The five chapter Portia Nelson story also points out the importance of our role in taking charge of our own lives. There are many tools at our disposal...all types of therapy, alternative medicine, Eastern and Western medicine, organic eating and healthy exercise.

Native healing always incorporates the mind, body, spirit connection.

The following statement is a *Native American Teaching* and is as follows:

*"We are all connected in the circle of life that never ends.*
*Since we are all connected in the circle of life, what happens to one,*
*happens to*
*All.*

*All things are created equally divine.*
*Since all things are created equally divine, all are teachers and*
*students.*

*Whatever I think, is!!!*
*Anything I wish, I create, I become, I do.*
*Everything has purpose!*

*We live parallel lives. (Both in this dimension and other dimensions).*
*Each day is one step closer to Source …Learning unconditional Love*
*for all parts of our soul. Parts meaning spiritual and corporeal*
*(physical) incarnations."*

Anyone who irritates you, creates a doorway through which you can learn a great lesson about yourself. Therefore, bless the person who irritates you for you could not ask for a greater gift than personal growth.

~

## Chapter 9- Self Esteem

The fourth level of Maslow's *Hierarchy of Needs* is self-esteem. Our self-esteem is based largely on the internal messages we give ourselves. These messages can stem from our upbringing, or our understanding of our external environment, as it relates to our perceptions of acceptance or rejection. Depressed people often tell themselves they are inadequate, their situation is hopeless, they are helpless, and nothing will change for the better.

Our self-esteem is based on the ratio of negative to positive things we say to ourselves in such internal dialogues. These thoughts often carry over into feelings of anxiety, shame, envy or frustration.

The chart on the next page is a list of many of our psychological needs, and the ineffective and effective ways we choose to meet them. Within the ineffective category, we see much evidence of low and questionable self-esteem, with the various ways a person may use to cover their inadequacy. This can serve as a diagnostic tool to determine where the dysfunctional loopholes are and how we can correct them. We would hope that seeing the ineffective need-meeting mechanisms, one would choose to change to the more effective methods in the third column.

**PSYCHOLOGICAL NEEDS**
**-CHOICES TO MEET THEM-**

| NEEDS | MEETING YOUR NEEDS INEFFECTIVELY | MEETING YOUR NEEDS EFFECTIVELY |
|---|---|---|
| SECURITY | Possessing things and/or people; controlling or being controlled by others. | Developing skills to take control; making decisions. |
| FAITH | Fanaticism; giving control away. | Seeing the positive; trust in self; believing without needing reasons. |
| WORTH | Angering; powering; criticizing; having to win. | Making a plan to achieve; taking risks; focusing more on process. |
| FREEDOM | Practicing self-denial; making excuses; trying to change others. | Making better choices; acting responsibly. |
| BELONGING/LOVE | Depressing; paining; giving only to receive. | Choosing to approach first; sharing; accepting others. |
| FUN/ENJOYMENT | Drinking and drugging; overeating; acting irresponsibly; waiting for others to make fun. | Being a fun-maker; seeing the world as a pleasurable place. |
| KNOWLEDGE | Thinking too much; memorizing. | Seeing more; brainstorming; seeing yourself achieving what you want. |
| HEALTH | Making excuses; inconsistent exercise; looking for instant change and results. | Being in balance in all needs; developing physical awareness. |
| YOUR CHOICE | Short term; feel good temporarily; weakness; work to be comfortable. | Long-term; feel good in long term; strength; work to be fulfilled. |

*(For enlarged image of this diagram go to page 89)*

An effective behavioral tool to begin changing your mind about how you fit into the world and raise your self-esteem is Assertiveness Training. The following statements may be helpful in determining whether that tool could be useful to you.

Here are the ***Assertive*** questions. Check if applies:

- ___Do you return faulty merchandise?
- ___Do you generally express what you feel?
- ___If someone keeps kicking or bumping your chair in a movie or lecture, do you ask the person to stop?
- ___In a good restaurant, when your meal is improperly prepared or served, do you ask the wait person to correct the situation?
- ___Are you able to openly express love and affection?

- ____Do you insist that a mechanic or repairman make repairs and adjustments which are his/her responsibility?
- ____Are you able to ask your friends for small favors or help?
- ____When you differ with a person you respect, are you able to speak up for your own viewpoint?
- ____Are you able to refuse unreasonable requests made by friends?

Here are the **_Non –Assertive_** questions. Check if applies:

- ____Do you continue to pursue an argument after the other person has had enough?
- ____Are you disturbed by someone watching you at work?
- ____Do you show your anger by name-calling or obscenities?
- ____Do you try to be a wallflower or a piece of furniture in social situations?
- ____Do you often step in and make decisions for others?
- ____Do you think you always have the right answer?
- ____Do you have difficulty complimenting or praising others?

Many of these questions may indicate other diagnoses, such as narcissism or anxiety. But the issues are the same, in terms of finding better, more effective ways to interface with others.

Assertiveness training can help, regardless of what else may be happening, in regard to stumbling blocks on the path to a healthy adjustment.

There are only four ways we interact with others.

1) Passive, which is really a non-interaction. Passive people "seem" to respect others, but not themselves.

2) Aggressive people "seem" only to respect self and not others.

3) Passive/aggressive people use a combination of both, where the aggressive person uses devious tactics to force the other person to agree with them or to get them to do what the passive/aggressive person wants. Passive and aggressive people present only in a manner that seems to respect self or others, but are not genuine about their respect at all.

4) Assertive people do genuinely respect both self and others. Assertiveness is the only authentic and positive interaction that contains no hidden agendas or lack of acceptance. Assertive people receive more acceptance and treat others with a positive, accepting attitude. These are often the most successful and comfortable people, as they navigate through their chosen journeys.

| | Assertive | |
|---|---|---|
| **Passive** | RESPECTS SELF AND OTHERS | **Aggressive** |
| SEEMS TO ONLY RESPECT OTHERS | Self-respect/self-esteem | SEEMS TO ONLY RESPECT SELF |
| Victims | Respects others | Guiltless |
| Shy/retiring | Self confidence | Critical |
| "yes" people | Win/Win | Manipulative |
| Fearful | Compromising | Victimizing |
| Angry (stressed) | More input | Inciting |
| Internal | Listening skills | Provocative |
| Withdrawn | Mutuality/commonality | Angry |
| Caretakers | Mature | External |
| Doormats | Mutually beneficial | Violating |
| Guilt ridden | Nurturing | Self-interested |
| Never wins | Deep, meaningful relationships | Immature |
| Overly apologetic | Emotionally healthy | Blaming |
| Acts-in (negative energy is stuffed inside) | Fair and equal | Acts out (negative energy directed to others) |
| | More choices | Never loses |
| | Self-assured | Never wrong |
| | Care-givers | Never apologizes |
| | Supportive | |
| | I'm OK; You're OK | |

*(For enlarged image of this diagram go to page 91)*

Practicing assertiveness, whether it is genuine or not, will help it to become integrated and become more and more the "Real" you. When one is able to achieve a genuine, assertive view of life, they can feel a new sense of health, happiness and well-being. The following is a modification of *12-step program affirmations*, which may also be helpful in self-concept improvement.

- Just for today, I will respect my own and other's boundaries.
- Just for today, I will be vulnerable with someone I trust.
- Just for today, I will act in a way that I would admire in someone else.
- I am a worthwhile person.
- I am a precious person.
- I am beautiful inside and outside.
- I love myself unconditionally.
- I have ample leisure time without feeling guilty.

- I deserve to be loved by myself and by others.
- I am loved because I deserve love.
- I am a child of God and I deserve love, peace, prosperity and serenity.
- I forgive myself for hurting myself and others.
- I forgive myself for letting others hurt me.
- I am capable of changing.
- The pain I feel by remembering can't be any worse than the pain I feel by knowing and not remembering.

Many people, in all cultures, believe that showing aggression is a positive stance. We are shown this on our playing fields, in politics, in schools and in our business dealings. Aggression "seems" to accomplish the desired ends. But it has been shown that more successes come from the respect shown in assertiveness, than the intimidation delivered by aggressive people. A certain amount of assertiveness is a necessary step in claiming our self-esteem, which can only keep rising as we feel better about ourselves. Passive people have no sense of control, even over their own decisions. Aggressive people like to feel in control of everyone and everything, even at the expense of others. But assertive people genuinely respect all, including the self, while engaging in productive intercommunication. The results are beneficial to all, not just the few.

Self-esteem equates to the independent stage of the Evolutionary Cycle from Chapter 6. The Independent stage of Separation/Individuation, and a congruent (inside and outside the same) sense of self will allow a person easy access to the next level of Self-Actualization.

Fall

## Chapter 10- Self Actualization

The fifth stage of Maslow's *Hierarchy of Needs* is self-actualization, which also corresponds to the independent stage on the Evolutionary Chart in Chapter 6. The independent stage is the stage of Separation/Individuation, enabling a congruent sense of self. Congruent meaning inside and outside the same, with no hidden agendas. Having successfully navigated the basic physiological needs, need for safety and security and the need for self-esteem, we are ready to experience our sense of self on a higher level…that of our own self-actualization.

The following characteristics are indicative of a congruent, high functioning, and relatively peaceful person:

1) Live close to reality - Perception of reality is comfortable and the individual has the ability to understand others more accurately and tolerate ambiguity and uncertainty. Reality can be perceived at face value through the "Real" and authentic self.
2) Accept self and others - They accept themselves and their various characteristics with little or no guilt and at the same time, can readily accept others.
3) Problem-centered - They are not ego-centered or self-interested, but often devoting themselves to broad social problems.
4) Spontaneous - Have the capacity to be spontaneous in both thought and behavior,

although they seldom show extreme unconventionality.

5) <u>Need for privacy</u> - Has frequent need for privacy, meditation, and solitude, thus, are capable of looking at life from an objective point of view.

6) <u>Independent of culture and environment</u> - They are not pressured or influenced by others, society, or culture and are capable of deciding on their own.

7) <u>Deep appreciation</u> - They enjoy and appreciate the basic experiences even if they have been experienced many times before.

8) <u>Deep social interest</u> - They identify in a sympathetic way with all people in general.

9) <u>Deep satisfying, and meaningful relationship</u> - Usually relate meaningfully to a few people rather than many.

10) <u>Democratic</u> - They relate to all people with an attitude of respect, regardless of race, creed or income level.

11) <u>Enjoy the means to the end</u> - They are able to discern between means and ends and enjoy the means better than more impatient people.

12) <u>Creative</u> - They have primary creativity that produces truly original, new discoveries.

13) <u>Own attitudes</u> - They fit into the culture, but make their own individual decisions.

14) <u>Mystical experiences</u> - Significant experiences such as feeling limitless horizons and authentic power. Peak experiences of deep positive feelings, consisting of deep appreciation and aesthetic perspectives.

All of these characteristics of a self-actualized person are, indeed, those of an enlightened, high-minded, loving and honest being. We all may know some people like this, or we look to people, past or present, who represent high and honest values and who advocate for all, not just a few.

The following "Personal Bill of Rights" may help in arriving at a higher level of being and understanding:

1) Life must have choices beyond mere survival.
2) You have a right to say no to anything when you feel you are not ready or it is unsafe.
3) Life must not be motivated by <u>fear</u>.
4) You have a right to all your feelings.
5) You are probably not guilty.
6) You have a right to make mistakes.
7) There is no need to smile when you cry.
8) You have a right to terminate conversations with people who make you feel put down and humiliated.
9) You can be healthier than those around you.
10) It is ok to be relaxed, playful and frivolous.
11) You have a right to change and grow.
12) It is important to change and grow.
13) You can be angry at someone you love.
14) It is important to set limits and know your opinions matter.
15) You can take care of yourself, no matter what circumstances you are in.

Author Unknown

A large part of our growth and development will come from spreading our wings and trying new things, as well as stretching ourselves in new directions. Many people fear taking chances or risks, for fear of repercussions. Consider this then…

- To laugh is to risk appearing a fool.
- To weep is to risk appearing sentimental.
- To reach out for another is to risk involvement.
- To place your ideas, and your dreams before the crowd is to risk their loss.
- To love is to risk not being loved in return.
- To live is to risk dying.
- To hope is to risk despair.
- To try is to risk failure.

But risks must be taken, because the great hazard in life is to risk nothing. The person who risks nothing, has very little to remember, to inspire, and to develop. They may avoid suffering and sorrow, but they simply cannot learn, feel, change, grow, love…live. Chained by their certitude, they are slaves.

They have forgone their freedom; only a person who risks is free.

With the desire and ability to change, grow, and expand one's knowledge base, anyone can reach a higher level of enlightenment, inclusiveness, and self-actualization.

Mother Theresa had an inscription written on her wall in Calcutta. It states...

*"People are often unreasonable, irrational, and self-centered.*
*Forgive them anyway.*
*If you are kind, people may accuse you of selfish, ulterior motives.*
*Be kind anyway.*
*If you are successful, you will win some unfaithful friends.*
*Succeed anyway.*
*If you are honest and sincere, people will deceive you.*
*Be honest and sincere anyway.*
*What you spend years creating, others could destroy overnight.*
*Create anyway.*
*If you find serenity and happiness, some may be jealous.*
*Be happy anyway.*
*The good you do today, will be forgotten.*
*Do good anyway.*
*Give the best you have and it will never be enough,*
*Give your best anyway.*
*In the final analysis, it is between you and God.*
*It never was between you and them anyway."*

The first time I heard this was in 1992 as a commencement address to my son's graduating class.

It made an impression on me, so I copied it and have often used it in my practice. It is memorable because, almost anything we do or try or use as innovation or experiment, will never please everyone. There will be "losses", but do it anyway, if only for your own fulfillment and enjoyment.
The beauty of the self-actualized person is the ability to persevere through challenges, obstacles, rejection and pain

to find the lesson intended to propel us forward. It is an achievement of great value that lasts a lifetime.

~

## Chapter 11- Transcendence

Transcendence is the spiritual identity that exists at our highest level of consciousness. It is the level of extending love, as opposed to crying out for love. It is love, not fear. It is forgiving yourself, by realizing that nobody can act beyond their level of consciousness, as emphasized by Eckhart Tolle, author of *The Power of Now*.

Ralph Waldo Emerson reflects on the meaning of success, in his poem of the same name.

SUCCESS

*"To laugh often and much:*
*To win the respect of intelligent people and the affection of children:*
*To earn the appreciation of honest critics and endure the betrayal of*
*False friends:*
*To appreciate beauty:*
*To find the best in others:*
*To leave the world, a bit better, whether by a healthy child, a garden*
*patch, or a redeemed social condition:*
*To know even one life has breathed easier because you have lived.*
*This is to have succeeded."*

Here, there is no mention of external power, money, judgment, shame, envy, greed, lust or any ego allurements. It is, instead, the peace, harmony and love that exists in one's heart that creates the success. You must consider what is truly in your heart. *The Course in Miracles* speaks of love... *"Love will enter immediately into anyone who wants it, but it must truly be desired. Your task is not to seek for love, but merely to seek and find all of the barriers within yourself that you have built against it. With love within you, you have no need for anything, except to extend it."*

Love is the deepest human and all-encompassing emotion that humans can feel.

Even the *Bible* quotes St Paul in stating… *"Love is patient; love is kind. It does not envy; it does not boast; it is not proud. It is not rude; it is not self-seeking, it is not easily angered; it keeps no records of wrongs. Love does not delight in evil, but rejoices with the truth. It always protects, always perseveres."*

If, in fact, love and its opposite, fear, are the only overall emotions we humans experience; then the only emotion we can embrace is love, if we wish to reach the higher levels of enlightenment. Both love and fear have a multitude of subcategories, such as love has joy, gratitude and grace, while fear has anger, vengeance and envy, to name a few. What might make it easier for us to remember the experiences of love and fear is to ask ourselves…Am I crying out for love, or am I extending love?  Transcended people exude an air of peace and serenity and have spent a lifetime loving others.  They have worked to erode any of those feelings of selfishness, pride, self-absorption, and exclusion.  Enlightened people are inclusive and assertive and approach all others with grace and dignity.  They have quieted the clamor all around and have mastered the technique of deep meditation. Serenity must come from the inside out and generally cannot be found in the everyday clamor and the turmoil of the outside world.  However, a peaceful person can find serenity wherever they seek…a falling leaf, a duck on a pond, a horse grazing in a field, a cluster of Aspen trees growing on the hillside, or a child's laughter. If there is clamor in their midst, they can remove themselves or "stand in the middle of the fire" and sustain themselves with their own inner peace.   Again, the *Course in Miracles* states:

"To love yourself is to heal yourself.  Sickness is a defense against the truth. I will accept the truth of what I am, and let my mind be wholly healed today.  Vision has power. This is the light that brings your peace to other minds, to share it and be glad that they are one with you and with themselves. This is the light that heals."

The most beautiful passage from *Gifts from The Course in Miracles* follows:

*"Beyond the body, beyond the sun and moon,*
*Past everything, you see and yet somehow familiar,*
*Is an arc of golden light*
*That stretches as you look*
*Into a great and shining circle.*
*And all the circle fills with light*
*Before your eyes.*
*The edges of the circle disappear,*
*and what is in it is no longer contained at all.*
*The light expands and covers everything, extending to infinity forever shining*
*And with no break or limit anywhere.*
*Within it, everything is joined*
*in perfect continuity.*
*Nor is it possible to imagine*
*that anything could be outside for there is nowhere*
*that this light is not.*
*Here is the meaning of what you are;*
*A part of this with all of it within,*

*And joined to all as all is joined in you.*
*Accept the vision that can show you this."*

The *Course in Miracles* is not a "how to" book, but instead, it is a statement of what we all are striving to accomplish in life. We all wish to feel encompassed in that golden light and feel the fullness of our love contributing to the golden light. If we do not feel that love and light, then we may be resisting it with fear and anger. Our job, then, becomes to look in the nooks and crannies to find the fear and barriers that hold us back and prevent the experience of light.

What may help to discover where some barriers may still exist, is to look at the following:

### SYMPTOMS OF A SPIRITUAL RECOVERY

- *A TENDENCY TO THINK AND ACT SPONTANEOUSLY, RATHER THAN OUT OF FEARS BASED ON PAST EXPERIENCES.*
- *AN UNMISTAKABLE ABILITY TO ENJOY EACH MOMENT.*
- *A LOSS OF INTEREST IN JUDGING PEOPLE.*
- *A LOSS OF INTEREST IN INTERPRETING THE ACTIONS OF OTHERS.*
- *A LOSS OF INTEREST IN CONFLICT.*
- *A LOSS OF THE ABILITY TO WORRY. (THIS IS A VERY SERIOUS SYMPTOM).*
- *FREQUENT, OVERWHELMING EPISODES OF APPRECIATION.*
- *CONTENDED FEELINGS OF CONNECTEDNESS WITH PEOPLE, PLACES, AND THINGS, ESPECIALLY NATURE.*
- *FREQUENT ATTACKS OF SMILING.*

- ***AN INCREASED TENDENCY TO LET THINGS HAPPEN, RATHER THAN MAKING THEM HAPPEN.***
- ***AN INCREASED SUSCEPTIBILITY TO THE LOVE EXTENDED BY OTHERS AS WELL AS THE UNCONTROLLABLE URGE TO EXTEND IT.***

*Recovery Trade Pub*

~

## Chapter 12- Conclusions

Abraham Maslow has uniquely orchestrated a framework of common human evolutionary processes that encompass all parts of humanity...mentally, physically, emotionally, and spiritually. His pyramid structure enables us to see the necessary steps in our reach for the apex of unconditional love and transcendence. There are neither mistakes nor regrets; there are only opportunities to learn and grow. Growth we must do, because transcendence is not a given; it must be studied and understood and skills will be developed in order to feel peace of mind. The pitfalls encountered along the pathway are a necessary part of the emerging process. I had one client tell me once, he was so glad he was a recovering alcoholic, because if he weren't, he would not be in the fellowship of AA and getting treatment for his illness. This is addressing the issue and learning to work it through, so it can be released. Denial is not a workable solution.

Mental Health is a positive state of balance whereby one is able to adjust to the ebb and flow of life, without over-reacting in negative or unhelpful ways. Mental health is a state of living in the present, not without relationship to the past or the future, but not driven by either.

Maintaining balance in a changing world is often a struggle and can consume much of our energies. When our security or our level of comfort is greatly disturbed through serious personal problems or, radical changes in our life, we can react by retreating and withdrawing, or we can see it as an opportunity for growth. It is helpful from time to reflect on our ways of approaching life and to access our state of mind.

The following Mental Health Inventory may be helpful in determining where some weak points may lie. Read each of the questions and grade yourself (on the line) from 0-10, where *10 is perfect*, no problem here; *0 is not so good*, below *5 would indicate an area of concern*.

Once you have scored all questions you will have an inventory of your state of mind.

- ____Do I enjoy an inner peace, relatively free of tension and anxiety, of moodiness and depression?
- ____Do I have the ability to adjust and stay flexible under stress, and to cope with tragedy, when necessary?
- ____Do I have the capacity to accept myself insofar as my unchangeable limitations are concerned, and to avoid competing neurotically?
- ____Do I get along well with my spouse? Have we kept our romance alive?
- ____Do I enjoy my children and give them the time I'd like to give and help them to mature happily? If they are older, have I encouraged their emancipation and do I continue a warm loving relationship with them?
- ____Do I have friends with whom I am comfortable?
- ____Do I treat others as individuals, understanding their needs?
- ____Do I invest myself in others?

- ____Am I active and productive, do I get things done and do I budget prudently the time and energy I have?
- ____Am I satisfied with the quality and the quantity of the work I do?
- ____Do I have multiple interests, and obtain my pleasures from many sources?
- ____Do I get more joy from giving, than getting?
- ____Do I have faith, a religion, or a philosophy of life, which means much to me?
- ____Do I assume responsibilities toward helping with the social needs that concern us all? Is my commitment beyond that of the average person?
- ____Do I contribute to the grace and beauty of my surroundings?
- ____Do I do what I can to keep myself interesting and attractive?
- ____Do I ever take the time to think about where I am and where I want to go?
- ____Do I re-evaluate periodically my priorities and my accomplishments?
- ____Do I take a long view of my future?
- ____Do I allow myself time for personal growth?
- ____Do I refrain from using alcohol or another drug to dull or enhance reality for me?
- ____Do I have the courage to seek help when I need it?

Review your answers. <u>If you have a majority of your answers at 5 or less there is the indication of a need to consider "inner child" work; working up through the first three stages of Maslow's *Hierarchy of Needs.*</u> (See Chapter 2). Here may lie many unconscious processes, of which we are unaware. At this stage, it is really up to us, our commitment, our perseverance and determination and how badly we want peace of mind. If we put ourselves at self-actualization, without really understanding the early experiences, we may fail at our pursuit of higher mindedness. The ancient Gnostic belief of "Know Thyself" is integral here, for we must understand our unconscious motivators. Thus, there could be a need to select a professional that can assist in facilitating this process.

I have been asked the question, "if I checked many items for the checklist of Hidden Anger (Chapter 7) and I scored low on the Mental Health Inventory above; What's next? What should I do?"

As one who is a professional, here is how I would approach the process with a client:

I would immediately look at the social conditions and environment they were born into. I would then look at the family of origin and any special conditions that existed for the individual. If you intend to work with a professional, I would choose one who utilizes a psychodynamic, holistic, approach, which uses historical, developmental material to track the early and later history, i.e. " Inner Child Work." This would proceed with looking at the history of early childhood and how it unfolded. Here, there may be a "working through" process to try to unravel issues that continue to plague you. As you begin to experience genuine self-esteem, either simultaneously or through alternative therapies... healing touch therapy, animal therapy, tapping therapy, body talk, yoga, acupuncture, dry needling and study of other belief systems, we will have a growing interest in moving to that higher level.

My belief involves a simple metaphor, involving the Three Component Mind, which I believe all humans have, regardless of whether the behavior is good, bad or indifferent. (1) Higher mind which is our love-based birthright; (2) Lower mind, which is the fear-based, unevolved part of the mind. I would call this the ego, only because it is fear-based, despite its necessity in protecting us and assisting in the daily chores of living. The third component, since we are born into a free-will zone, is the (3) Decision-maker, who chooses between lower and higher mind. These three components make up our apparatus for navigating the world in which we live.

My metaphor involves an auto with three people...driver, and two passengers. In the driver's seat, we most often put the ego, because ego has always driven and motivated our comings and goings. In the front passenger seat is decision-maker, who makes decisions on who drives and how and where to drive, and then higher mind will often either be in the back seat or the trunk, never to interfere in our process that motivates us forward, unless called upon. Now, if we can imagine that the fear-based ego is only evolved to the three year old level, one has to wonder why it is driving a difficult vehicle. We see this example every day in immature driving or road rage and wonder why? If we can remember who quietly sits in the back seat, waiting for some recognition that, for many, never comes. At this point, we must choose again and replace lower with higher mind and put it in the driver's seat. This is our opportunity to choose again, change our mind and recognize that an unevolved part of the mind should not be behind the wheel or motivating us through the higher levels of our life's journey. Granted, this is an extreme example, but it says what might be helpful, if we take notice of our journey and how we are handling it.

An example might look like this:

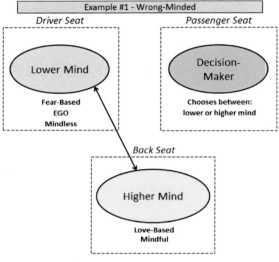

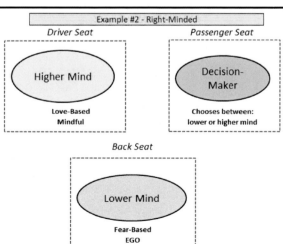

Let's review the four evolutionary principles which are so integral to the our growth:

1) The human purpose on Earth is to evolve physically, emotionally, mentally and spiritually.
2) Every human being has a Divine Essence made of light and love, whose nature is goodness.
3) Free will is an absolute universal right; impeccability calls on the self to surrender its free will to divine will in faith and trust.
4) All of natural existence is sacred beyond how it serves or meets the needs of the individual self.

We now have a more successful and meaningful journey back to the sea through the ascending stages of Maslow's Hierarchy of Needs. I can promise you a more enthusiastic and loving journey in all of life's encounters.

> *"It is now time for you to dwell in*
> *the House of eternal LOVE*
> *and play in the garden called heaven*
> *on the earth of your creation.*
> *We are waiting for you."*

P'TAAH

~

MARILYN BROOKHART

# Epilogue-

Congratulations! Hopefully, you have successfully navigated a journey back to the sea, the Oneness, the place of peace and harmony. The tiny drop of sea water has now found its way back home or at least, is moving in a favorable direction to reach for the place of peace. The journey now becomes easier and pleasanter as we join with Source and Oneness. The most prominent feeling is unconditional love and respect for all of life's forms. The *Course in Miracles* would say life on earth is an illusion created by us to experience separation from our Source. The separation was made by us, into a classroom, of sorts, in order to learn and have opportunities to grow into deep and meaningful enlightenment. How we do this and how we reach the higher levels of enlightenment is strictly up to us. There are many pathways and choosing to avail oneself of the many roads can be useful, in order to find what works for you. Inevitably, they will all cross paths and end in the same place. They all converge at some point, providing they are love oriented and not negatively based. Negativity and judgment are generating only dark energy that serves no one. Learning is the major, most important reason for being here… to learn that this is a journey that brings us closer to the Oneness. What affects one, affects us all. As Chief Seattle says in one of his famous quotes… "Earth does not belong to us; we belong to the earth." He goes on to say that "Humankind has not woven the web of life. We are but one thread within it. Whatever we do to the web, we do to ourselves. All things are bound together. All things connect. We are part of the earth and the earth is part of us."

Enjoy the ride! It's made for you and keeps the journey, a happy one.

~

For a guided mediation led by Marilyn Brookhart, please visit her YouTube channel.
**www.YouTube.com/MarilynBrookhart**

# Appendix- enlarged diagrams-

## Reference: Page 46:

| ROLES | VISIBLE QUALITIES | INNER FEELINGS | REPRESENTATION TO THE FAMILY |
|---|---|---|---|
| Family Hero | Receives positive attention<br>High achiever<br>Visible success<br>Does what's right | Inadequate<br>Inferior<br>Guilty<br>Some narcissism | Family's self-worth<br>Structure<br>Stability<br>Family pride |
| Scape Goat | Receives negative attention<br>Hostility<br>Defiance<br>Anger<br>Acts out | Hurt<br>Guilt<br>Abandonment | Deflects focus away from the dysfunctionality<br>"Squeaky Wheel" gets the negative attention |
| Lost Child | Withdrawn<br>Loner<br>Follower<br>Trouble making decisions<br>Invisible | Loneliness<br>Powerlessness<br>Unimportant<br>Suicidal<br>Depressed | Relief<br>One child family doesn't have to worry about |
| Mascot/Clown | Fragile<br>Immature<br>Joker<br>Hyperactive<br>Learning disabled | Fear<br>Anxiety<br>Stressed | Comic relief<br>Fun and humor<br>Lightens load |

Reference: Page 58:

## PSYCHOLOGICAL NEEDS
### -CHOICES TO MEET THEM-

| NEEDS | MEETING YOUR NEEDS INEFFECTIVELY | MEETING YOUR NEEDS EFFECTIVELY |
|---|---|---|
| SECURITY | Possessing things and/or people; controlling or being controlled by others. | Developing skills to take control; making decisions. |
| FAITH | Fanaticism; giving control away. | Seeing the positive; trust in self; believing without needing reasons. |
| WORTH | Angering; powering; criticizing; having to win. | Making a plan to achieve; taking risks; focusing more on process. |
| FREEDOM | Practicing self-denial; making excuses; trying to change others. | Making better choices; acting responsibly. |
| BELONGING/LOVE | Depressing; paining; giving only to receive. | Choosing to approach first; sharing; accepting others. |
| FUN/ENJOYMENT | Drinking and drugging; overeating; acting irresponsibly; waiting for others to make fun. | Being a fun-maker; seeing the world as a pleasurable place. |
| KNOWLEDGE | Thinking too much; memorizing. | Seeing more; brainstorming; seeing yourself achieving what you want. |
| HEALTH | Making excuses; inconsistent exercise; looking for instant change and results. | Being in balance in all needs; developing physical awareness. |
| YOUR CHOICE | Short term; feel good temporarily; weakness; work to be comfortable. | Long-term; feel good in long term; strength; work to be fulfilled. |

89

Reference: Page 61:

| Passive | Assertive | Aggressive |
| SEEMS TO ONLY RESPECT OTHERS | RESPECTS SELF AND OTHERS | SEEMS TO ONLY RESPECT SELF |
| --- | --- | --- |
| Victims | Self-respect/self-esteem | |
| Shy/retiring | Respects others | Guiltless |
| "yes" people | Self confidence | Critical |
| Fearful | Win/Win | Manipulative |
| Angry (stressed) | Compromising | Victimizing |
| Internal | More input | Inciting |
| Withdrawn | Listening skills | Provocative |
| Caretakers | Mutuality/commonality | Angry |
| Doormats | Mature | External |
| Guilt ridden | Mutually beneficial | Violating |
| Never wins | Nurturing | Self-interested |
| Overly apologetic | Deep, meaningful relationships | Immature |
| Acts-in (negative energy is stuffed inside) | Emotionally healthy | Blaming |
| | Fair and equal | Acts out (negative energy directed to others) |
| | More choices | Never loses |
| | Self-assured | Never wrong |
| | Care-givers | Never apologizes |
| | Supportive | |
| | I'm OK; You're OK | |

# References-

*P'Taah: The Gift* by Jani King

*A Time to Heal* by Timmien L Cermak, MD

*Love, Medicine and Miracles* by Bernie Siegel, MD

*Psychology of Life* by Philip G. Zimbardo

*The Laws of Spirit* by Dan Millman

*The Therapist's Handbook* by Benjamin Wolman

*Object Relations and the Developing Ego in Therapy* by Althea Horner

*Codependent, No More* by Melody Beattie

*The Course in Miracles*

*Self-Esteem* by Virginia Satir

*Homecoming* by John Bradshaw

*Stages of Psychological Development* by Eric Ericson

*Hierarchy of Needs* by Abraham Maslow

*The Holographic Universe* by Michael Talbot

*Transcending the Levels of Consciousness* by David Hawkins, MD

*Cover photo credit: Tom Bry*

*Interior photos proprietary to Brookhart Enterprises, LLC*

Made in the USA
Middletown, DE
21 September 2016